RED-HOT BIKES
DUCATI

Clive Gifford

W
FRANKLIN WATTS

This edition 2012

First published in 2007 by
Franklin Watts
338 Euston Road
London NW1 3BH

Franklin Watts Australia
Level 17/207 Kent Street
Sydney NSW 2000

Series editor: Adrian Cole
Series design: Big Blu
Art director: Jonathan Hair

A CIP catalogue record for this book is available from the British Library.

ISBN: 978 1 4451 0735 6

Dewey Classification: 629.227'5

Acknowledgements:
The Publisher would like to thank Ducati UK
All images © Ducati Motor Holding S.p.A.
The Publisher acknowledges all © names as the property
of their respective owners.
Every attempt has been made to clear copyright. Should there be any
inadvertent omission please apply to the publisher for rectification.

Printed in China

Franklin Watts is a division of Hachette Children's Books,
an Hachette UK company.
www.hachette.co.uk

Contents

In 1926, three Ducati brothers, Bruno, Marcello and Antonio, formed the Ducati company in Italy. At first, the company produced radios and electrical items. After World War II (1939–45) it started to produce small motorised bicycles.

⬆ *Leaning into the bend, this rider is testing a Ducati 1098 out on the racetrack.*

Full throttle facts

Company name: Ducati Motor Holding, S.p.A.
Year of founding: 1926
First bike model: Cucciolo

Employees: 1,172 (2008 figures)
Headquarters: Bologna, Italy
CEO: Mr Gabriele Del Torchio

Cutting-edge design

Ducati's first biking success was the Cucciolo – a bicycle with a small motor and two-speed gearbox that was sold from 1946 to 1958. Fabio Taglioni joined Ducati in 1954 as a young but ambitious engineer. He became responsible for many of Ducati's cutting-edge designs.

↑ *Fabio Taglioni (standing on the far right) admires the Ducati 750.*

↑ *Former world champion Troy Corser does a wheelie on his Ducati 916.*

Racing and riding

Over the years, Ducati has grown to become one of the world's leading producers of high-performance motorbikes. They are used on the road and on the racetrack. In fact, Ducati's motto for their bikes is: "Try It On The Racetrack First". Today, Ducati produce a wide range of bikes that all share the company's dedication to styling and superb performance. In this book you will get up close to six of Ducati's most exciting and popular motorbikes.

Number of bikes sold: 35,000 per year
Number of models: 22

Best-selling model: Monster
Number of manufacturing plants: 1

The Italian word Multistrada means "many roads" in English, and the Multistrada, or MTS 1100, is designed to cover exactly that. It can perform well in many different riding conditions. It is a motorbike as comfortable on dirt tracks as on regular roads. The MTS comes in two models: the standard 1100 and the 1100 S – a sports version.

More power

The very first version of the Multistrada was released in 2003 with a 992 cc engine. Two years later a smaller bike with a 620 cc engine was produced. For 2007, Ducati increased the engine's size to 1078 cc. The Multistrada 1100's engine generates 95 bhp, more than some small hatchback cars.

The Multistrada 1100 handles winding mountain roads easily.

Engine configuration

The number of cylinders an engine has, and the pattern they are laid out in, is called the engine configuration. Ducati builds many of its engines with two cylinders, known as twins. The layout of these cylinders varies. The MTS 1100 has its cylinders arranged at a 90-degree angle, called a V-twin (or L-twin) configuration.

Full throttle facts

Top speed: 215 kph (estimated)
Wheelbase: 1,462 mm

Power output: 95 bhp
Fuel capacity: 20 litres

↑ The Multistrada 620 out on the open road. The bike features an upright riding style, which is comfortable for touring and riding the machine over long distances.

The chassis of the Ducati MTS 1100 is made of tubular steel. This makes the bike very strong and reduces the bike's weight

↑ Here a Multistrada 1100 has been stripped down to reveal its frame, which is made of tough, tubular steel.

Kerb weight: 196 kg
Seat height: 850 mm

Engine capacity: 1078 cc
Gearbox: 6-speed

Rider comfort

Vibrations from the wheels rolling over a road or track can travel up through many motorbikes' frames. These jolt the rider's hands on the handlebars. Over a long distance this can make riding very tiring. Both the Multistrada 1100 S and the 1100 feature vibration-isolated handlebars to reduce this movement. The bodywork of the front of the bike is split into two sections. A lower fairing covers the front of the bike and holds the front headlight. The upper part is a windshield that turns with the handlebars, offering the rider wind protection when travelling at high speeds.

↑ You can see the windshield above the front fairing in this photo.

MTS 1100 / S (Multistrada)

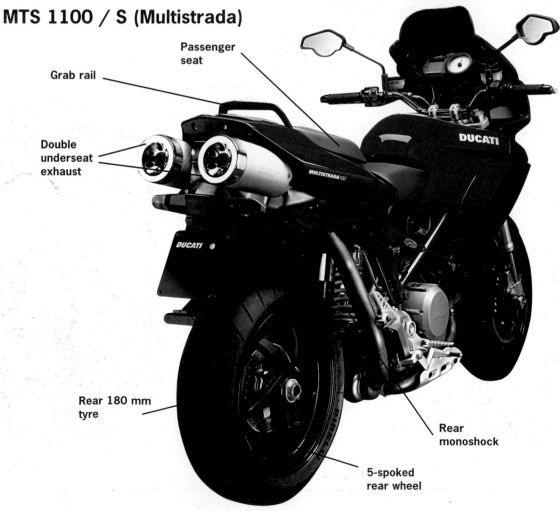

Passenger seat

Grab rail

Double underseat exhaust

Rear 180 mm tyre

Rear monoshock

5-spoked rear wheel

Shock absorbers

Shock absorbers are adjustable cylinders connected to the wheel axles. They travel up and down as the bike moves, absorbing some of the shock or impact of riding over dips, ruts or bumps. The Multistrada 1100 features a pair of front shock absorbers and a single shock absorber, known as a monoshock, for the rear wheel. This rear shock absorber is adjustable depending on the load the bike is carrying and the riding conditions.

Tech talk

Axle – the central shaft that a wheel spins round.

Fairing – a shell, usually made of plastic or fibreglass, fitted over the frame of some motorbikes to direct the air around the bike and rider.

Trellis – a strong, cross-over pattern.

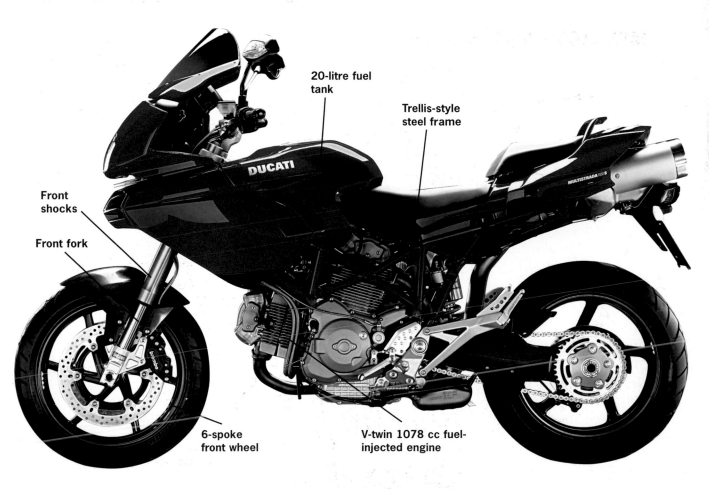

20-litre fuel tank

Trellis-style steel frame

Front shocks

Front fork

6-spoke front wheel

V-twin 1078 cc fuel-injected engine

Wheelbase measures 1,462 mm

The 1098 is the successor to Ducati's famous 999 Superbike, which raced in the World Superbike Championships up until 2006. It won the title three times. The Ducati 1098 is almost 14 kg lighter, but comes with an engine that is 100 cc larger and generates around 20 bhp more than the 999 it replaces.

Borrowed from racing

Some of the technology in the Ducati 1098 was developed from Ducati's experiences on the racetrack. This includes the machine's powerful disc brakes and the all new Testastretta Evoluzione engine. It is the most powerful twin-cylinder motorbike production engine in the world.

This Ducati 1098 (left) is the current World Superbike model. Number 21 is ridden by Troy Bayliss.

Full throttle facts

Top speed: 281 kph (estimated)

Wheelbase: 1,430 mm

Power output: 160 bhp

Fuel capacity: 15.5 litres

Clear display

The Ducati 1098 has an instrument panel with no buttons on it. Instead, the large LCD display is controlled by a switch on the handlebars. It shows a range of information, including bike speed, engine speed given in revolutions per minute (rpm), oil temperature and pressure, fuel level and average speed and fuel consumption. The bike and engine speed can be shown in numbers or as a bar graph across the screen.

⬆ This is a close up of the instrument panel showing the bar graph speed indicator.

⬆ A rider takes the Ducati 1098 through its paces. The bike's riding position helps the rider tuck in behind the fairing. This avoids buffeting from the air and helps maintain speed.

Tech talk

Disc brake – a brake system where brake pads press onto a disc attached to the motorbike wheel, slowing and stopping the wheel from turning.

LCD – liquid crystal display; a type of screen (many flat-screen TVs now use LCDs).

Production engine – an engine built in large numbers for sale in vehicles available to the general public.

Kerb weight: 173 kg
Seat height: 820 mm

Engine capacity: 1099 cc
Gearbox: 6-speed

Sports version

Currently, the 1098 comes in three different versions – the standard model, the 1098 S sports model and the Tricolore (shown below). The 1098 S is tuned for maximum performance and weighs 2 kg less than the standard bike. It comes with a data analyser package that collects information about the last ride, such as maximum speed and engine performance. This information can be collected by a USB key and put on a personal computer for the rider to check.

⊕ *The Tricolore is the 1098 S, finished in a stunning green, white and red colour scheme that matches the Italian flag. It also comes with a racing engine control unit (ECU) and a racing exhaust muffler kit that increases power.*

Drive chain

The drive chain is a chain of metal links, similar to a bicycle chain, that transfers the power from the motorbike's engine to the rear wheel. The chain turns the gear cog, called a sprocket, which is fitted to the rear wheel axle. This moves the rear wheel round.

Ducati 1098

Fuel tank includes a 4.1-litre reserve tank

Rear light

Twin exhausts made of stainless steel

Front 330 mm brake disc

Rear wheel, with 5 spokes that are Y-shaped for strength

V-twin 1098 cc engine

Drive chain

Rear 245 mm brake disc

Twin headlights

Front wheel suspension allows the wheel to travel up and down a maximum of 127 mm

Tech talk

ECU – short for engine control unit, a computer that controls many of the engine's functions.

Muffler – also called a silencer; the attachment at the end of the exhaust system that helps to reduce engine noise.

USB – short for universal serial bus; a way of connecting electronic devices to a personal computer.

The Monster 695 is the latest version of Ducati's Monster 'naked' street bikes. These are bikes stripped of all bodywork that isn't essential, such as the front fairing. As a result, the twin-cylinder engine can be seen clearly.

Monster models

The first Monster, the 900, was unveiled in 1992 at a motor show in Germany. It caused a sensation with its aggressive design. In 1994 Ducati released a smaller model, the 600, and in 1998 they produced the 600 Dark. It had an entirely matt-black finish, allowing owners to customise their bikes. Before the arrival of the 695, over 170,000 Monsters had been sold all over the world.

⊕ *Here you can clearly see the 695 cc fuel-injected engine of the Monster 695 on full display.*

Full throttle facts

Top speed: 201 kph (estimated)
Wheelbase: 1,440 mm

Power output: 73 bhp
Fuel capacity: 14 litres, including 3 litre reserve

Waste reduction

The waste engine gases, or emissions, from the Monster 695 pass through an exhaust system that includes two catalytic converters. Electronic sensors make sure that the bike releases as few harmful gases into the atmosphere as possible. The gases finally pass through a pair of oval-shaped silencers, made of aluminium, which help to reduce the noise of the gases leaving the bike (see page 17).

⊕ *The Monster 695 has the lowest seat height of any Ducati currently available.*

Tech talk

Aluminium – a strong, lightweight metal.

Catalytic converter – also called a 'cat', this device removes most poisionous gases, or emissions, from an engine's exhaust, before they are released into the air.

Customise – to modify a motorbike, for example by painting it a different colour.

Fuel injection – a system that carefully controls the amount of fuel entering an engine cylinder.

Naked – a class of motorbike that has very few fairings.

Kerb weight: 168 kg
Seat height: 770 mm

Engine capacity: 695 cc
Gearbox: 6-speed

Cylinders and pistons

When air and fuel are ignited (set alight) in an engine cylinder, the expanding gases created push a piston up and down a cylinder. The movement of this piston is harnessed to drive a motorbike's rear wheel round. Life for a cylinder piston is fast and furious, pumping up and down at extreme pace and pressure. The engine in the Monster 695 is designed to allow the pistons to travel 17 per cent slower than the previous Monster bike, the 620, while not affecting performance. This helps to make the engine more reliable.

Monster 695

Front indicator lamps

Large front headlight

Front 3-spoke wheel

Front 300 mm diameter twin disc brake

HOT SPOT

Slipper clutch

A clutch is the device that enables gears to be changed when riding. A slipper clutch is designed to slip slightly when a motorbike rider changes down the gears and brakes sharply. Its aim is to make slowing down safer and more comfortable, and to stop the rear wheel locking, which might cause the bike to skid over. Slipper clutches are normally found on competition bikes, but the Monster 695 also has one, called an Adler Power Torque Clutch.

Accessories

A range of accessories are available for the Monster 695, including a leather racing outfit and a matching seat cover and fairing set, which can be fitted to the bike. The engine can also be boosted with an engine performance kit. This includes a pair of lightweight carbon-fibre exhaust silencers, a new air filter, and an engine control unit designed to maximise engine performance.

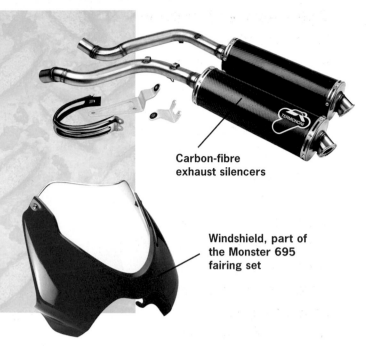

Carbon-fibre exhaust silencers

Windshield, part of the Monster 695 fairing set

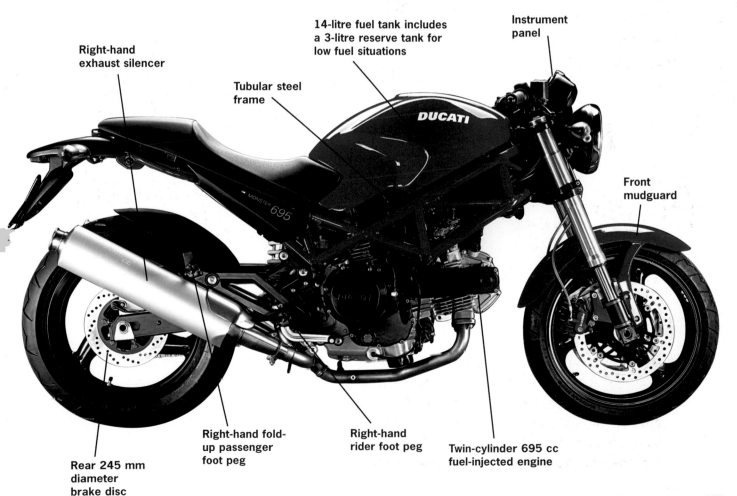

Right-hand exhaust silencer

Tubular steel frame

14-litre fuel tank includes a 3-litre reserve tank for low fuel situations

Instrument panel

Front mudguard

Rear 245 mm diameter brake disc

Right-hand fold-up passenger foot peg

Right-hand rider foot peg

Twin-cylinder 695 cc fuel-injected engine

Ducati ST3 / ST3 ABS

Sports touring motorbikes offer high performance that can be maintained over long distances. Ducati's latest sports touring motorbike comes in two versions, the standard ST3 model and the ST3 ABS, which features anti-lock brakes and five-spoke wheels. It also has an upside-down front fork that is fully adjustable for different loads and riding conditions.

⬆ *The Ducati ST3 carries a passenger and luggage comfortably.*

Full throttle facts

Top speed: 241 kph (estimated)

Length: 1,430 mm

Power output: 102 bhp

Fuel capacity: 21 litres

Touring traditions

Touring on a motorbike means long-distance riding and the need for comfort and storage. The Ducati ST3 has handlebars that can be adjusted in height and an advanced on-board bike computer that calculates fuel and range. The exhaust pipes can also be adjusted in height. They can be raised up to allow the rider to lean over further into bends, without the bike body touching the ground. They can also be set to a much lower position, so that the bike can be fitted with a pair of panniers for storage.

HOT SPOT

ABS braking

Sometimes, when a rider applies the brakes hard, the rear wheel may lock and stop turning, and the bike may end up slipping or skidding. Anti-lock braking systems (ABS) feature sensors that monitor a wheel's speed. A computer determines whether the brakes should be eased off or on for a moment to prevent wheel lock. On the ST3 ABS, the rider can turn the ABS system off for a sporty ride.

Tech talk

Panniers – storage cases or boxes made to fit on the sides of a motorbike.

Sensors – devices that measure something around them, such as speed of movement or temperature.

Kerb weight: 201 kg	**Engine capacity:** 992 cc
Seat height: 820 mm	**Gearbox:** 6-speed

Three valve, twin cylinder

The ST3 is powered by the Desmo 3 engine. This is a liquid-cooled, twin-cylinder powerplant with fuel injection. Each cylinder has three valves that help keep fuel consumption low but also allow plenty of power to be generated. When running at 8,750 rpm, the Desmo 3 can generate a hefty 107 bhp.

Cylinders

Ducati ST3 / ST3 ABS

Front fairing
with clear
windshield

Dual beam
headlight

Air vent

Left indicator
lamp

Front tyre
120 mm wide

Tech talk

Fuel consumption – the amount of fuel an engine uses.

Rpm – short for revolutions per minute; a measurement of the speed of an engine.

Valve – a device that opens and closes to control the flow of fuel in an engine.

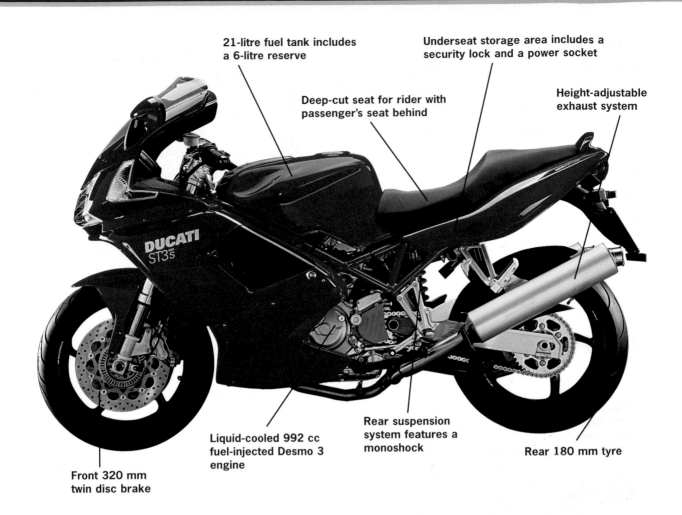

21-litre fuel tank includes a 6-litre reserve

Underseat storage area includes a security lock and a power socket

Deep-cut seat for rider with passenger's seat behind

Height-adjustable exhaust system

Liquid-cooled 992 cc fuel-injected Desmo 3 engine

Rear suspension system features a monoshock

Rear 180 mm tyre

Front 320 mm twin disc brake

Wet clutch

The clutch is the mechanism that allows a rider to switch up and down gears on a motorbike. The ST3, like many motorbikes, has a wet clutch system. The moving parts of the clutch are covered in oil. This helps to keep their temperature down when the bike is running, as well as reducing wear and tear on the parts. A wet clutch is quiet and hard wearing. It is expected to last well over 100,000 km.

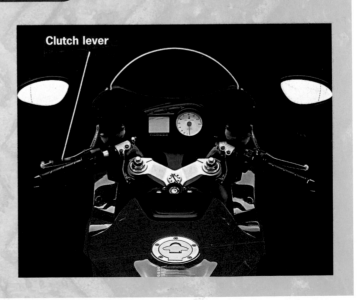

Clutch lever

In the 1970s, Ducati released a series of GT (Grand Touring) bikes that captured the imagination of many motorbike enthusiasts. These bikes included the legendary 1971 Ducati GT 750 bike designed by Fabio Taglioni (see page 5). The GT 1000 is a modern classic, designed to capture the spirit of the 1970s.

⬆ The Ducati GT 1000 is a bike designed to look like those from the past, but is packed with modern 21st century features.

Full throttle facts

Top speed: 216 kph (estimated)
Length: 1,425 mm

Power output: 91 bhp
Fuel capacity: 15 litres

⬆ *These riders are making the most of the power generated by the GT 1000's 992 cc engine.*

Tech talk

Acceleration – an increase in speed of a motorbike.

Chrome – a silver-coloured metal used for its attractive, mirror-like appearance.

Enthusiast – describes someone who has a strong liking or interest.

Immobilizer – a device that stops thieves from stealing a motorbike by preventing the engine from being started without a key.

Classic styling

The GT 1000 is packed with traditional-looking features, from chrome twin exhausts and spoked wheels to lots of polished aluminium and chrome details. These include the fuel cap, wheel rims, handlebars, and the trim around the instrument panel. The slim fuel tank features depressions called knee cut-outs on the sides, which help to create a comfortable riding position.

Kerb weight: 185 kg
Seat height: 828 mm

Engine capacity: 992 cc
Gearbox: 6-speed

Fuel efficiency

For a large and powerful motorbike generating almost 100 bhp, the GT 1000 is relatively fuel efficient. In regular riding it can manage approximately 17.7 km per litre. So, a full 15-litre tank can propel the bike for up to 265 km. The instrument panel on the GT 1000 includes a trip-fuel function. This allows the rider to check how many kilometres of fuel are left in the tank.

Ducati GT 1000

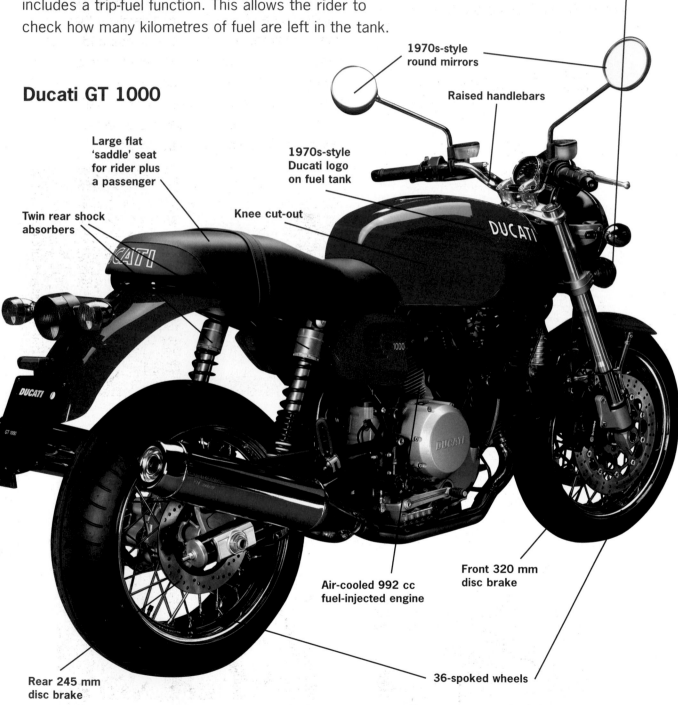

Right-hand chrome-covered horn

1970s-style round mirrors

Raised handlebars

Large flat 'saddle' seat for rider plus a passenger

1970s-style Ducati logo on fuel tank

Twin rear shock absorbers

Knee cut-out

Air-cooled 992 cc fuel-injected engine

Front 320 mm disc brake

Rear 245 mm disc brake

36-spoked wheels

Clothing and accessories

To complete the classic 1970s look, a large range of accessories are available for the GT 1000 owner. These include the following:

Sportclassic helmet

Monster Dog sunglasses produced by Oakley and Ducati

CAD

The GT 1000 has a classic look, but it is packed with up-to-date features and was developed using computers. CAD is short for Computer Aided Design. It involves the use of powerful computers to shape and design parts on screen, and then to run a series of tests, called simulations, to see how the parts and the bike perform. CAD is used to help design many motorbikes, including all those in Ducati's range.

Leather gloves

Smart boots with toe, ankle and heel protection

Classic-designed leather jacket

25

Ducati Desmosedici RR

The Desmosedici RR is the first ever road-going motorbike to offer the stunning performance and technology taken directly from MotoGP. The RR is a road-going version of the Desmosedici GP7. The GP7 is a new version of the bike that Loris Capirossi and Sete Gibernau used in the 2006 MotoGP World Championship. The attention to detail is so great that this limited edition motorbike is being produced at a rate of just 400 machines a year.

⬆ *Blink and you'll miss it – this is the racing version of the Desmosedici RR, called the GP7.*

Full throttle facts

Top speed: 340 kph (estimated)

Wheelbase: Information not available

Power output: 200+ bhp

Fuel capacity: 21 litres (estimated)

Return to MotoGP

At the start of the 21st century, rule changes in Grand Prix motorbike racing encouraged Ducati to return to the MotoGP competition. The bike they built, the GP3, took part in the 2003 competition. Its successor, the GP4, managed a top speed record of 347.4 kph when ridden by Loris Capirossi in testing in Spain. In 2006, Ducati motorbikes won four of the seventeen MotoGP races, with Loris Capirossi finishing third in the MotoGP World Championship. The latest version is the GP7. It is ridden by Loris Capirossi and Casey Stoner.

⬆ Ducati riders Loris Capirossi (second from left) and Casey Stoner (third from left) pose with team members in front of the Desmosedici GP7 bike in an Italian ski resort.

Kerb weight: 165 kg (estimated)
Seat height: Information not available

Engine capacity: 989 cc
Gearbox: 6-speed

Massive power

Most Ducati bikes have twin-cylinder engines. The engine of the Desmosedici RR, like the other Desmosedici machines, features a 4-cylinder engine with an aluminium crank case and titanium connecting rods. This engine can run at staggering speeds. Whilst many bikes can handle 7–9,000 rpm, the Desmosedici RR's engine can run at an incredible 17,000 rpm. The engine generates a huge amount of power, in excess of 200 bhp!

HOT SPOT

Desmodromic valves

Ducati's latest high-performance bike is named after desmodromic valves, a technology Ducati has used on their motorbikes since the 1950s. Air and fuel enter an engine's cylinder through a valve, and the exhaust gases leave from another valve. In many engines, the opening of the valve relies on a spring. This can sometimes lead to a drop in accuracy and performance at high engine speeds. Desmodromic valves have no spring, and control both their opening and closing with pinpoint accuracy and smoothness.

Handlebars surrounded by body fairing

Bodywork made of tough but lightweght carbon fibre

Front twin 320 mm disc brake

Ducati Desmosedici RR

Fuel tank made of aluminium alloy

Sculpted racing seat, supported by a carbon-fibre frame

A 4-2-1 exhaust system (four pipes leave the engine, one for each cylinder, then run into a single exhaust pipe) hidden under the tail

Rear brake lights

Drive chain

Liquid-cooled 4-cylinder 989 cc engine (hidden under fairing)

Bridgestone tyres designed especially for the Desmosedici RR

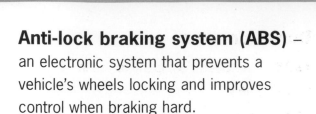

Anti-lock braking system (ABS) – an electronic system that prevents a vehicle's wheels locking and improves control when braking hard.

Brake horsepower (bhp) – a unit of measurement used to describe the power generated by an engine that is used to move a bike or other vehicle.

Carbon fibre – a flexible, lightweight material made of strands of carbon heated and stretched together.

cc – short for cubic centimetres, it is used as a measurement of the size of the engine's cylinders.

Cylinders – the places in an engine where fuel and air are ignited to generate power.

Drive chain – similar to a bicycle chain, it is a chain that transfers power from the engine to the rear wheel.

Fairing – a shell, usually made of plastic, fitted over the frame of some motorbikes to direct the air around the bike and rider.

Foot pegs – rests or short poles that stick out from the sides of a motorbike and give riders somewhere to place their feet.

Fuel injection – a device that forces fuel directly into an engine, producing rapid acceleration.

Handling – how a motorbike responds when being ridden, such as how it turns into and out of corners.

Kerb weight – the total weight of a motorbike with standard equipment and liquids, including oil, coolant and a full tank of fuel, but not with a rider.

Monoshock – a single shock absorber, found on the rear of a motorbike, not on the front.

Piston – a disc that moves up and down inside an engine cylinder.

Shock absorbers – devices that are designed to absorb sudden forces and impacts to the suspension of a vehicle.

Suspension – the system of springs, shock absorbers and other components, directly connected to the wheels or the axles to help create a smooth ride.

Touring – travelling over a long distance.

Wheelbase – the distance between the front and rear axles on a motorbike.

Websites

www.ducati.com
The official website of Ducati, with information on the latest models and racing performances.

http://www.ducati.com.au/
The website for Ducati bikes in Australia and New Zealand.

http://www.ducatisportingclub.com/
The UK Ducati owners and riders website with galleries of bikes and details of events around the country and abroad.

http://www.ducatisuite.com/history.html
An interesting look at the history of some of Ducati's most famous and important motorbikes.

Books

The Ducati Story: Road and Racing Motorcycles from 1945 to the Present Day
Ian Falloon (Haynes Group, 2011)
A thorough guide to the company's development and its leading bikes.

The Ducati Monster Bible
Ian Falloon (Veloce Publishing, 2011)
An indispensible guide to Ducati's best-selling model – the Monster – charting its evolution since the 1990s.

Museo Ducati: Six Decades of Classic Motorcycles from the Official Ducati Museum
Chris Jonnum (David Bull Publishing, 2012)
Illustrated with stunning photographs, this book profiles 25 historic motorbikes from Ducati's official museum in Bologna, Italy.

Ducati 1098/1198
Marc Cook (David Bull Publishing, 2010)
A behind the scenes look at Ducati's "make or break" motorbike, the 1098. The book includes interviews, bike sketches and hundreds of photos.

Ducati timeline

1926 – The Ducati company forms in Bologna, Italy.

1946 – Ducati introduces a 4-stroke 48 cc clip-on engine for bicycles, the "Cucciolo" or "pup" in Italian.

1954 – Fabio Taglioni is appointed technical director of Ducati.

1955 – Ducati's first true racing bike, the Gran Sport Marianna, is developed.

1972 – Ducati introduces the V-twin Desmo and the 750 SuperSport.

1980 – First Ducati Pantah-engined bike goes on sale.

1989 – Fabio Taglioni retires from Ducati.

1990 – Raymond Roche on a Ducati 851 wins the World Superbike Championships.

1993 – The first Ducati Monster motorbike goes on sale.

1995 – The 916 SBK Superbike debuts.

2001 – Ducati MH900e becomes the first motorbike to be sold only on the Internet.

2003 – Ducati bikes totally dominate the World Superbike Championships, winning all 24 races. Ducati re-enter the MotoGP competition after a gap of 30 years.

2006 – After being owned by Americans, Ducati returns to Italian ownership. Ducati also win the World Superbike Manufacturers and Riders Championships.

2011 – A new Ducati superbike, the 1199 Panigale, is released.

Index